Bibliographic information published by the German National Library:

The German National Library lists this publication in the National Bibliography; detailed bibliographic data are available on the Internet at http://dnb.dnb.de .

Imprint:

Copyright © 2014 GRIN Verlag
Print and binding: Books on Demand GmbH, Norderstedt Germany
ISBN: 9783668837478

This book at GRIN:

https://www.grin.com/document/449841

Sebastian Simbeck

Cormac McCarthy's "The Road". Social Interactions and Social Relations

GRIN Verlag

Universität Paderborn

Fakultät für Literaturwissenschaften

Institut für Anglistik und Amerikanistik

Sommersemester 2014

Cormac McCarthy's *The Road*:

Social Interactions and Social Relations

Sebastian Simbeck

Lehramt Gy/Ge: 1.Englisch und 2.Geschichte (LPO 2003)

"Maybe you'll be good at this. I doubt it, but who knows. The one thing I can tell you is that you won't survive for yourself. I know because I would never have come this far. A person who had no one would be well advised to cobble together some passable ghost. Breathe it into being and coax it along with words of love. Offer it each phantom crumb and shield it from harm with your body." (McCarthy, *The Road* 57)

"Action is rational in so far as it pursues ends possible within the conditions of the situation, and by means, which, among those available to the actor, are intrinsically best adapted to the end for reasons(...)." (Parsons, 1937: 58)

These two epigraphs, the first from Cormac McCarthy's *"The Road"* and the second from Parsons *"Structure of Social Action"* give us a slight hint about the importance of social relations and interactions and their outcomes. As a consumer of this kind of post-apocalyptic media you're thrown into these settings by either waking up from a dream or by regaining consciousness. The setting and the "new world order" are already fixed. Either people try to survive for their own while searching and hoping for "others" in order to have a higher chance of surviving, or they are already a part of a community which fights against others in order to survive. In both cases, on the other hand, those "communities" already do exist and in both cases it's always a question of the "good" against the "bad". While dealing with post-apocalyptic media several questions came to my mind. How came those communities and groupings and into being? Which role do social interactions and social relations play in order to form a new kind of social system(s), after the (previous-) known world-order got destroyed by an apocalyptic event? Social sciences usually deal with the reasons of social interactions and relations. But they depend on existent fixed social values, rules, laws, morale and religious believes, since those aspects influence the actions of each and every individual. In this essay I'd like to take a look at social interactions of individuals who find themselves in a world where known values, believes and rules seem to be invalid and where the individual survival seems to be the only aim to strive for. But is survival the only need of people? *The Road*, with its cold, bitter and ashen world, where ethics and morale are lost, where "society", as we know it, is completely absent is a good basis for this research.

2

"The science or study of the origin, development, organization, and functioning of human society; the science of the fundamental laws of social relations, institutions, etc."
(http://dictionary.reference.com/browse/sociology)

Sociology deals with the relationships between individuals and with 'social interactions' which is the building block of society. 'Social Interaction' can be defined as an exchange of two or more individuals by using symbols. Those symbols are interpreted and lead to another social action. A behavior, for example a single movement, is defined as an as soon as it conveys meaning. When it's addressed to someone else it's a form of social behavior. A social action is given as soon as you expect a reply from the one you just addressed. The next step would be a social contact, which means you do receive a response, a form of interaction. Do these steps happen repeatedly 'social interaction' takes place. These social interactions can only take place in in social groups. (vgl. *Abels, Einführung in die Soziologie*). George Simmel, a German sociologist and philosopher described in is pioneering work on pure social forms a 'dyad' (two members) as the smallest form of a social group, followed by a triad (three members) and, of course, lager social groups do exist where these social interactions happen repeatedly. Within those groups the members try to define rules, and design a morale which they seek to live. It's quite obvious that those may differentiate in various perspectives. Microsociology tries to study social interactions and Ethnomethodology, a sub-branch of it, questions how people's interactions can create the illusion of a shared social order despite not understanding each other fully and having different perspectives.

"From the point of view of sociological theory the moral order consists of the rule governed activities of everyday life. A society's members encounter and know the moral order as perceivedly normal courses of action-familiar scenes of everyday affairs, the world of daily life known in common with others and with others taken for granted. They refer to this world as the 'natural facts of life' which, for members are through and through moral facts of life" (Garfinkel 1967, 35).

In order to proof his thesis he conducted several experiments which aimed at destroying this 'social order' which basically means the constitutive expectation one has. He did this by choosing a 'victim' who got confronted with the actions of a cooperation partner who acted against all constitutive expectations in a specific discourse. If the first person's actions are not matching up to the second's expectations, Garfinkel believes that the second person would have difficulties to understand the sense of the first persons actions, since every action needs to be rule-governed. Possible reactions might be fear, disorientation, being perplexed or indignation. Every kind of social interaction therefor depends on rule-governed constitutive expectations which are used as an assumption for the interpretation of the behavior of other participants. Talcott Parson, an American sociologist, on the other hand described, regarding to individuals, values are the meanings which are contributed to things and actions. He mentioned that all kinds of social systems derive from the interaction of individuals as a unity.

"Values are modes of normative orientation of action in a social system which defines the main directions of action without reference to specific goals or more detailed situations or structures." (Parson 1958, S.171)

He claims that values and norms (Ethics) are the essential factors which assure social order. The only question here is of how institutional preconditions of society are to be linked with subjective motivations of agents. Erich Fromm, a German psychologist, sociologist, humanistic philosopher said:

"In order that any society may function well, its members must acquire the kind of character which makes them want to act in the way they have to act. (…) They have to desire what objectively is necessary for them to do. Outer force is to be replaced by inner compulsion." (Fromm, 1944, S. 381)

As you can see many theories do exist about the function of social-systems. The problem here is, and that's why I started this essay the way I did, that most theories have significant gaps and other sociologist try to fill these gaps by introducing another theory, but none of them can explain or grabs the exact relation of subjective motivations, existent social systems, or ethics. Instead of skipping theory to theory I'd like to use the finding mentioned above while taking a closer look on "The Road".

4

Throughout the book "The Road" there are several social interactions within byads, triads, and other (bigger) social groups, that can be analyzed and interpreted. On the one hand we have the father and his son, which we follow throughout the book. We get to know about their social values, their morality, their rules and their ways of thinking, how they integrate in the new social order of the world.

They represent the "good" guys, which seem to be absolutely absent in this horrible world of hate, ignorance and individual struggles, a world with its own rules. On the other hand we get to know about "others", various other unknown groupings or single individuals, which seem to be the "bad" guys. It soon becomes clear that each and every form of grouping has different expectations, ways of living, attitudes and behavior towards foreigners which lead to the fact that we as readers define it as the "good" and as the "bad" guys. Since the organization, and the functioning of a generalized human society are completely absent in this novel there are still aspects to observe which indicated a somewhat like a shared social order. The only problem here is that we just have a limited point of view, since we just get to know about other groups by the descriptions of the byad, the father and son relationship, "each the other's world entire"(6).

"Bye and bye they came to a set of tracks cooked into the tar. They just appeared. He squatted and studied them. Someone had come out of the woods in the night and continued down the melted roadway. Who is it? Said the boy. I don't know Who is anybody."(49)

This is the start of very first situation where the father and the son are personally confronted with the "others." While reading this short paragraph above the importance of being careful within this post-apocalyptic world becomes obvious. The father and the son already developed a certain ritual when they see other signs of life. The father first "studied" the tracks and analyzed their direction. The son on the other hand, fully relying on his father asks who that is. By answering "Who is anybody" the father indicates that everybody has lost his identity. Identity describes *"who a person is, or the qualities of a person or group that make them different from others"(http://dictionary.cambridge.org/dictionary/british/identity)* The depth of these words becomes more clear if we think about identity as a social term. During my research I learned that in sociology identity arises of belonging to social groups, by adapting habits, rituals, ways of thinking or values and morals. The identity is formed by selecting aspects of specific cultures for oneself. This indicates that identity closely is connected to social groups which interact on a fixed

5

set of common social order. By saying "who is anybody" therefor the father indicates, that no common social order does exist, so that everybody, even the father, has no identity. If we rethink the son's question "Who is it?" the son indirectly asks for the foreigner's identity, therefor his social belonging and therefor for the foreigners attitude and his intentions. They keep observing the man in order to find out more. After observing that the man is "dragging one leg slightly and stopping from time to time"(49). the father says "We're all right, Let's just follow and watch." He knows that this man is no danger to them and that's why they just follow him to "take a look, the boy said. Yes. Take a look"(49). Both, the father and the son, are not the ones who actively confront others but they are interested in other people. "As they passed he looked down. As if he'd done something wrong"(50). Here the man on the other hand, who is not a member of this dyad, therefor not knowing about their shared values, tries to avoid a confrontation. His situation is explained, too. He seems to be wounded, strucked by lightning, destroyed by the harsh world he is living in. It can be seen as the fate of "anybody" living by one's own.

> "Cant we help him? Papa? No. We cant help him. They boy kept pulling his coat. Papa?
> he said. Stop it. Cant we help him Papa? No we cant help him. There's nothing to be done
> for him. They went on. The boy was crying. He kept looking back"(50)

Even within this smallest form of group-formation there are several situations which show the difficulties in social interaction, as soon as personal experience and opinions differ from each other. In this paragraph, which describes the dyads further actions, we learn a lot more about the social interaction that takes places between the father and the son. Both individuals, the father and the son, have different pre-experience which influence their actions. The father knows about the lost world-order, of a pre-apocalyptic world, as it used to be. The son on the other hand just knows about this world by his father's stories and he therefor has a limited view about the circumstances as they are right now. The father has a specific concept in mind when it comes to morale, social rules, laws and good behavior. Not just from the past but also from the world they're living in right know. With his responsibility to protect his son from the "bad" and to keep both alive, he sees more, knows more and is the one who makes decisions. As I already pointed out above with Garfinkel's Theorie of Ethnomethodology, those experiences affect their actions in daily encounters with each other and, most importantly with foreigners. The problem in this situation is that the boy would like to help this man in any kind of way, to interact with him, to group up and to support each other. The father denies his request by saying "There's nothing to be done for him." Both have a different point of view here. The father knows about the man's fate and that he is dying soon. His observations, his rational way of thinking and his personal experience speak against helping this man, since "There's nothing to be done for him." The boy on the other hand does not fully understand his father's point of view, that's why he kept on asking a second time whether they're able to help and soon started to cry after his father denied his request.

The second situation where we get to know about this complicated social order can be found on the pages 60ff. where the father and son got confronted with a Roadrat as a part of a large group of scavengers. The father was woken up by any noise. "He raised his head slowly, the pistol in his hand"(60). Yet the father does not know what or who woke him but he is very precautious by grabbing his pistol. Again the father first observed the situation before taking any action.

"(...) when he looked back toward the road the first of them were already coming into view. God, he whispered. (...) "The boy was frozen with fear. He pulled him to him. It's all right, he said. We have to run. Don't look back. Come on."(60-61)

In comparison to their first personal confrontation here the father's reaction differs very much. He acts curious and the son's fear demonstrates the danger of each and every confrontation. While knowing about these dangers his father is saying: "It's all right." This can either be interpreted as an attempt to calm his son down, or as a hint, that this kind of behavior is kind of normal to them. "It's all right. (...) We have to run." This on the other hand shows us, that the dyad (son and father), which is a form of social group, is afraid of this large grouping, knowing about the differences between both of them, knowing about possible consequences when they are seen. This reaction of running away is therefore an action guided by pre-experience of the father. Later in the text a confrontation was unavoidable. A member of this larger grouping was too near to them which forced the father to take a first action, cocking a pistol. The following conversation (p. 63 to 66) is the best example for the difficulties in social interaction in this unnatural world.

7

"Are you a doctor? I'm not anything. We got a man hurt. It'd be worth your while. Do I look like an imbecile to you? I don't know what you look like"(64-65).

This excerpt shows that both, the man and the father, know about their different social belonging, and that their experience of the previous world order is invalid for both of them. "Are you a doctor? I'm not anything." Clearly demonstrates this fact. Now both do belong to another group having fixed rules and habits. "I don't know what you look like." implies that even the foreigner is not able to categorize the father properly. This leads to the fact that both, the father and the foreigner distrust each other.

"I'll bet that boy is hungry. Why don't you all just come on to the truck. Get something to eat. Aint no need to be such a hard-ass."(65)

The father denies this offer by saying they do only need a head-start and suddenly this situation escalates. The man gets shot and the father and son run for their lives. Again previous experience and knowledge about the harsh world made the father decide against this offer, whether this was the right decision or not, we'll never know. But what we do can say is, that the father and the foreigner both had to play a game, in which they had to find out about the opposites intentions. Depending on the outcomes of each and every social interaction a new social action was made. The result off all the previous interaction was "I think you're chickenshit"(65) which made him drawing his knife, grabbing the son. This finally lead to the fact that the father he "fell back instantly and lay with blood bubbling from the hole in his forehead"(66). Unnecessary to say that this social interaction had a negative outcome and that it had no influence to the development of a new social order. This whole situation gets even more interesting if we rethink this situation and what might have happened when the father would have trusted the man. The *"firm belief in the reliability, truth, or ability of someone or something"*, as the definition of trust according the oxford dictionary suggests, is not to be found here, which makes the interactions between two social groups impossible. In another example we get to know about marchers, "Dressed in clothing of every description, all wearing red scarves at their necks. Red or orange, as close to red as they could find." (91) This clearly indicates, that other kinds of groupings do exist, with their own values and their own social order, now even indicated with the usage of reddish scarfs symbolizing the membership of this social group. They do not only different in their outward experience but also in their social values and their morale.

8

"Behind them came wagons drawn by slaves, (...), some of them pregnant, and lastly a supplementary consort of catamites(...)"(92)

This clearly shows the difference between the dyad of father and son, and the lager group. The father and the son always try to help others, whereas this group keeps their own slaves. The father here again tried to protect his son by saying "Keep your face down. Don't look."(91) The father who failed to protect his son the last time does not want him to even look at the others. He tries to keep him silent and again both of them just observe the action taking place near them. The son does not know about much about other people. *"Were they the bad guys? Yes they were the bad guys. There's a lot of them, those bad guys. Yes there are. But they're gone"(92)* The son profits out of his father's experience by learning more about the world as it is. This effect of learning takes place within social groups permanently. In this scene it again becomes obvious that in The Road there are other, bigger groups existent with their own fixed social orders, having other values.

During the whole novel the father and the son are cautious when it comes to personal encounters with others. Sadly, the father did not make it until the end, to experience the last encounter the son is going to make. After his father died *"He stayed three days and then he walked out to the road and he looked down the road and he looked back the way they had come. Someone was coming. He started to turn and go back into the woods, but he didn't. He just stood in the road and waited, the pistol in his hand" (281).* This shows us, that the son is very different from his father. He learned by his father about the good and the bad guys, and their usual reaction would be to hide and to observe. He decides against it, just holding a pistol in his hand as a kind of last escape. He is brave enough to face the situation, while hoping for best things to come. This willingness and his believes in the coherent good in people make him act the way he does. After he decided to stay in that very place he still ignored the first hints for a "bad guy". He looked like *"A veteran of old skirmishes, bearded, across his check and the bone stoven and the one eye wandering. When he spoke his mouth worked imperfectly, and when he smiled."(281-282)* " As these lines demonstrate, individuals can hardly be rated by their outward appearance, only if you let them come closer get to know about their intentions. The father and the son had just some shared rules and values within their own little social group, so to say a code for The Good Guys: "Don't steal, don't eat people, don't lie, keep your promises and help others". *(vgl.* Erik J. Wielenberg. *God, Morality, and Meaning in Cormac McCarthy's The Road)*

9

Are you one of the good guys? [...] He looked at the sky. As if there were anything there to be seen. He looked at the boy. Yeah, he said. I'm one of the good guys."

The little boy then went on asking several questions where he tried to verify these rules. In the end he had no other choice to trust and to believe the men. *"How do I know you're one of the good guys? You don't. You'll have to take a shot"(283).* Finally he did and he got accepted in the foreigner's social organization, in form of a family. The book ended with some blank pages which leave every question open, still seeking for the end of this story.

Whether or not social groups fit to each other is hard to find out and seems to be an impossible task in a world were social values, rules, laws and other ethic believes are not valid. The father's wife, who shot herself early pointed out the difficulty and the impossibility of this new social order and therefor the last hope for human mankind. *"As for me my only hope is for eternal nothingness and I hope it with all my heart"(58).* She had the same realistic point of view as the father had, but he did not give up finding a solution, wandering through the deserted landscape with its thick blanket of ash. The father was not able to trust the words of others, so that his dyad stood alone in the end. The son on the other hand ignored all of these previous experiences and just let it happen, his only escape being the gun which he holds in his hand. The positive outcome of this by ignoring coexistent rules, here the behavior of his father as soon as they meet others, is the only way to break out of this isolation. This brings me back to Garfinkel's theories, as pointed out above: "Possible reactions might be fear, disorientation, being perplexed or indignation"

"You are kind of weirded out, aren't you?"(283)

Works Cited

Abels, Heinz. *Einführung in die Soziologie [Lehrbuch.* Wiesbaden: VS Verl. für Sozialwiss, 2007. Print.

Fromm, Erich. *Individual and Social Origins of Neurosis.* In: American Sociological Review, Vol. IX, 1944.

Garfinkel, Harold. *Ethnomethodological studies of work.* London New York: Routledge & K. Paul, 1986. Print.

Heritage, John. *Garfinkel and ethnomethodology.* Cambridge Cambridgeshire New York, N.Y: Polity Press, 1984. Print.

http://dictionary.cambridge.org/dictionary/british/identity (28.05.2014, 15:31)

http://dictionary.reference.com/browse/sociology (27.05.2014, 17:31)

Lamnek, Siegfried. *Qualitative Sozialforschung Lehrbuch.* WeinheimBasel: Beltz, 2010. Print.

McCarthy, Cormac. *The road.* New York: Vintage International, 2007. Print.

Schneider, Wolfgang L. *Garfinkel, RC, Habermas, Luhmann.* Wiesbaden: VS Verl. für Sozialwiss, 2005. Print.